What This B D0460158

By the time you've finished reading this book, you'll be able to describe the special behaviors of truly difficult people; you'll identify ways in which *you* evoke some of the difficulties you experience; and you'll learn some ways to change your own behavior and the effective communication skills that can help you handle problem people— maybe even win them over. So read on . . .

Other Titles in the Successful Office Skills Series

HOW TO
Deal
with
Difficult
People

DONALD H. WEISS

amacom

AMERICAN MANAGEMENT ASSOCIATION

This book is available at a special
discount when ordered in bulk quantities.
For information, contact Special Sales Department,
AMACOM, a division of
American Management Association,
135 West 50th Street, New York, NY 10020.

Library of Congress Cataloging-in-Publication Data

Weiss, Donald H., 1936–
     How to deal with difficult people.

     (The Successful office skills series)
     Includes index.
     1. Conflict management.   2. Interpersonal
relations.
3. Interpersonal conflict.   I. Title.   II. Series.
HD42.W45   1987   158'.2   86-47827
ISBN 0-8144-7674-0

Printing number

10 9 8

CONTENTS

Introduction

Difficult People

"Sometimes Kathy makes me so angry I'm ready to lose my cool—in front of Bryan, Virginia, God, and everyone."

Ever say anything like that? I bet you have.

No matter how well you get along with people, once in a while you run into someone with whom nothing seems to work. He or she seems to take perverse pleasure in *not* getting along with you.

And as luck would have it, you face that person regularly. He or she falls into a category of person you *can't* avoid: your boss, a peer, a customer, a supplier, a relative.

Of course, from your perspective, the fault is all his or hers. Right? As far as you know, you're not doing anything to evoke the contrary behavior.

Well, don't count on it. You can't always know how something you say or do—unawares—may trigger another person's contrariness. Now if you're unaware of how you might disturb someone else, chances are that difficult people also don't realize how what they say or do riles you. They may not even realize you're upset with them.

Furthermore, each of those difficult people may provoke you in a different way. One may be loud and egocentric, unwilling to let you connect in some cooperative or productive way. Another may sit back and glower, never really telling you what he or she thinks or feels. Another might talk your ear off, not getting much accomplished and not letting you get on with your work either.

Then some people mope about all the time or run around too much or swing in moody cycles. Others play games and try to manipulate everyone or try to go around them. How do you handle all these people?

If you don't know now, then after you've read this book, you should be able to recognize which ones are truly difficult people, as opposed to ordinary people who once in a while and temporarily become hard to get along with. You'll be able to describe the behaviors that most frequently create barriers to good relations.

You'll be able to recognize some of the things you do or say that evoke some of the difficulties you experience with others. You'll also learn some ways to change your own behavior, and some important, effective communication skills—listening, explaining, giving and getting feedback, achieving closure. Perhaps you'll also be able to win them over, get them to change their behavior, too.

Chapter 1

Who's Difficult—and Why

Kathy and Bryan report to Allen. They are all bio-chemists. Virginia is a production supervisor assigned temporarily to Allen's product development team. Allen is talking with his friend and colleague Sara, the product manager who takes up where the team leaves off. All these fictitious characters work for the equally fictitious Alexander's Frozen Foods Corporation.

Though I concocted the story, I didn't entirely invent the people. Each one represents a composite of many real people—people you'll recognize from your own experience. They depict behaviors commonly found in any workplace, in any walk of life. I created them to make otherwise abstract concepts concrete.

To Allen, Kathy's a "pompous, arrogant, know-it-all" with whom neither he nor anyone else "can argue rationally or even get in a word edgewise." That makes her—for him—a difficult person.

"Of course, Bryan's no help," Allen complains. "He sits there like a bump on a log, swallowing his pride, letting Kathy run right over him. No matter how hostile he gets, he rarely says anything. And as little as he talks, that's how much Virginia does.

"I need her on my team because she's a production supervisor, but she drives me crackers with her chatter and her kowtowing, especially to Kathy.

"Oh Lord, what did I do to deserve this motley crew?"

Usually, Sara sits and listens empathetically whenever Allen vents some frustration or another, but this time she responds. "The way I see it, it's not a question of what you *did* as much as what you plan to do about it." Smart woman, that Sara. "Sometimes you sound like Bryan," she adds. "Angry, but too passive to tell Kathy what you think. Your doing nothing may be part of the problem." Very smart woman.

Allen isn't through complaining. "Those soy patties have to be in production in two weeks, and we're nowhere close. They still dry out and crumble in the microwave. Every time someone opens his or her mouth, Kathy jumps into it with both feet, and we can't solve any of the problems we have. If something doesn't change soon, we're in deep trouble."

"So, boss, what are you going to do about it?"

Still beside himself and unsure of what he can do, Allen answers lamely, "All three of them are the most difficult people I know."

Probably so, for Allen, but in all fairness, they may not be difficult for someone else. Besides, everyone is hard to get along with in some way, under some circumstances, and with some people. You lose your temper sometimes; you withdraw other times; you cave in too easily in still other situations. That doesn't make you difficult, does it?

Sometimes the organizational climate where you work evokes the worst behavior in everyone. People often respond in kind to an authoritarian, bureaucratic climate. Sometimes, when the pressure becomes too threatening, they withdraw. The circumstances dictate the response.

Limited resources in an organization—money for raises, opportunities for promotions, and the like—create pressures that lead to competition. The competition often explodes into outright conflict. Under those conditions, some people become Mr. Nasty Hyde, while at home and in more satisfying surroundings, they're a regular Dr. Pussycat Jekyll. Their friends or relatives don't recognize them when you describe their on-the-job behavior.

So the first step is to separate the behavior from the individual and deal with the organizational climate as well as with the other person. The techniques I'll develop in this book will help you handle the person. Dealing with the organizational climate may be beyond your control. If you do have some power to influence the climate, encourage as many people as possible to develop the skills you'll learn here.

What is it that makes Kathy, Bryan, and Virginia *difficult,* while you, Allen, Sara, and I are only sometimes hard to get along with?

What's a Difficult Person?

Someone *periodically* hard to get along with *usually* isn't what would be defined as a difficult person. Special circumstances produce special behaviors. You have financial problems, your child is sick, your spouse loses his or her job. You get bitchy or crabby—or you get down in the dumps. Everyone who knows you says the same thing Sara says to Allen: "It's not like you to act this way."

That's the key difference. It's not like most people to act in a way that puts off other people and makes them feel they can't work with them or get along with them. Coping with someone's normal ups and downs is easier than coping with difficult people. By distinguishing between them and separating one type of behavior from another, you become empathetic to someone suffering some transient difficulty and take appropriate action with a truly difficult person—one whose behavior *regularly* interferes with your ability to get along with him or her and/or get your work done effectively or on time. The difficult person seems to you to be completely unmanageable.

In an earlier paragraph, I said that Allen's antagonist is difficult *for him.* In the definition above, I said "interferes with *your* ability . . ." and "seems to *you.* . . ." In sum, except in special cases, the difficulty is *in your relationship,* not necessarily *in the person or people.* It's a matter of how you and the other(s) in the relationship *perceive* one another and how much *tolerance* you have for one another's behavior.

Once you come to accept one another as you are and for what you are, you can use means for dealing with one another effectively. You can cope with the behavior(s) you at first found *difficult.*

After all, someone else may get on just fine with people you find impossible. Kathy's happily married. Bryan's engaged and has a close, intimate circle of friends. And Virginia's boyfriend finds her charming (though at times her kowtowing gets on his nerves, too). In each case, at least on the surface, someone, somewhere finds the person acceptable or manageable.

And didn't Sara point out that Allen may be difficult for the others (too passive when he should be assertive, thereby interfering with the group's ability to get on with its work)? Sara, too, may do something that interferes with someone else. Impossibility, like beauty, is in the eye of the beholder—most of the time.

Still, people can be difficult in one of two ways. They may be impossible or difficult *for you. You* feel a real need for creating change. Or *most of the people around them* may find them impossible or difficult. Then, *you and everyone else affected* feel a need for creating change.

Regardless of to whom a person appears difficult, the difficulty results from the two of you trying to fulfill your desires or meet your needs in different ways, from holding different opinions, from acting on different attitudes, from having different goals and values. Both of you want conflicting payoffs from your relationship or from the work situation in which you're both engaged. What separates you from the other person is that he or she is *unwilling* to yield, or to accept feedback, or to confront issues—at least, so far.

The techniques I'll describe later usually work to change all that. First, let's take a look at how those people interfere with us and at some of the whys.

Chapter 2

A Matter of Behavior

I've defined a difficult person in terms of behaviors for a reason. The adjectives *aggressive, passive,* or *too talkative* refer to character traits over which no one has much, if any, control. When dealing with a difficult person, that kind of name-calling only makes matters worse.

The process of real change begins when you recognize that the only person over whom you exercise any significant control is yourself—and you know what it's like to try to change yourself, your personality. When you break an old habit, you don't change some deep-seated character trait. Breaking a habit usually comes down to not doing something you typically do (not lighting up another cigarette, not taking another drink) or doing something you typically don't do (writing a daily "to do" list, making a log of your activities). Not doing or doing something is a behavior, not a trait.

Expect no more from other people than you expect from yourself—*a willingness to try to change their behavior* in relation to you, not to change their personalities. The degree of their willingness increases in proportion to the amount of influence you have with them, not necessarily as a boss but also as a friend or colleague.

Often what you call a person's personality is really a

pattern of behavior. Everyone exhibits a dominant pattern under most circumstances. Other times, when under pressure, people use a backup pattern, as well—a fallback position, so to speak.

Behaviors that *usually* get in the way of smooth working relationships or produce obstacles to getting along or stimulate conflict fall into three basic patterns with which you can deal fairly easily. Other, more outrageous behaviors you encounter require special attention and may not be amenable to easy change.

The Appendix is a short (unscientific) self-evaluation instrument you can use for identifying some of your own behavior patterns—ways in which you might act under certain circumstances. Complete part 1 of this exercise now. You'll get a chance to score the results after you've read what they mean.

Four Basic Patterns of Everyday Behavior

Behaviors can be summarized in terms of four basic patterns, the last three of which reflect behaviors of difficult people: *in-control and responsive* to other people (Allen, usually, and Sara); *in-control and unresponsive* (Kathy); *not-in-control and responsive* (Virginia); *not-in-control and unresponsive* (Bryan). Since Allen, along with Sara, can serve as positive role models, I'll start by describing what Allen *usually* does to be effective in coping with other people.

In-control/responsive. People who usually follow this pattern practice what can be called self-actualizing behaviors: They accept challenges; work well by themselves; look for ways in which to grow and to help others grow, as well; and enjoy the role of leader, but in an unobtrusive way. Allen and Sara represent self-actualizers who preserve their independence, influence, dominance, challenge, and recognition by acting reasonably, calmly, flexibly, and with caring for other people. They also feel enough self-esteem so as not to have to *demand* the esteem of other people. Self-recognition, self-satisfaction both suffice. Recognition by others takes second place.

They lead with openness and receptivity to other

people, listening to them, encouraging them to participate in the group's activities and decision-making process, and acknowledging their feelings. Both of them control through mutual respect and draw out the enthusiasm and creativity of the other members rather than requiring obedience to their will. As centers of communication, the ones to whom everyone else turns for accurate information, they quash rumors by getting at the facts and seeing to it that everyone else learns of them.

Within his team, Allen usually *sets goals* and helps everyone plan logically and in order of priorities. Well organized himself, he helps others implement their plans. His openness and honesty usually evoke openness and honesty in return. He's known in the group as a *gatekeeper* and *enabler,* getting group members to participate and to contribute on their own initiative.

By gatekeeping, Allen gives everyone an opportunity to exercise *personal power,* to feel competent and capable of meeting his or her own needs, whatever those needs may be. Team members then feel they have some control over their lives, though Allen's the team leader. This behavior style—assertive or proactive behavior—in itself creates no barriers to effective relationships. Allen gets himself into trouble not from his usual self-actualizing, proactive pattern but rather from his *backup pattern*—not-in-control/unresponsive.

By letting his team members exercise their personal power, Allen gives everyone the opportunity to act in his or her own personal interest, as well, which may not be congruent with the interests of the group as a whole. When the behaviors of other people interfere with success, people like Allen tend to let their personal perfectionism produce intolerance for any flaw in their own character or work. Doubling his effort not to stifle discussion by confronting his people, Allen withdraws. Reluctant to vent his frustration with the people from whom he's feeling resistance, he tends to let things get out of hand.

Allen's use of mutual respect as the basis of control sometimes fails because some of his team members don't respect one another and resist his attempts to get work done. He has allowed them to ignore ordinary work protocols in the interest of satisfying personal needs.

In-control/unresponsive. Whereas Allen tries to control assertively, Kathy wreaks havoc with the group through *aggressive* behavior. Yet striking similarities exist between Allen's and Kathy's controlling behavior. They differ dramatically in the quality of *how they respond to other people* while exercising their control.

Both seek independence or freedom to do their work without close supervision, influence, dominance, challenge, and recognition. This particular woman, however, feels threatened by anything that frustrates her wishes, and she becomes argumentative, haughty, pompous, and grating.

Kathy exercises her control without heeding the needs of others. She dictates to them, giving unsolicited advice and counsel, and then consolidates her personal power by denying other people their right to theirs. When someone else asserts himself or herself, Kathy becomes more aggressive, doing and saying things to call attention to herself. She attempts to lead the group whenever she can, frequently wrestling with Allen for power.

At the same time, Kathy takes on difficult tasks. Of course, when she rises to a challenge, she wants a lot of notice for her accomplishments.

This can be called "one-er" behavior: the belief (right or wrong) that "I'm one of a kind." One-ers demand rather than earn recognition. You can see why the barrier Kathy creates frustrates Allen so much. She refuses to enter into any meaningful *two-way* communication with anyone.

Bryan and Virginia, on the other hand, are easily pushed into submission, especially by Kathy. While both seek security (or safety), they represent two different types of passive behavior, both of which create their own barriers to successful operations. Bryan beats a hasty, hostile retreat when he feels threatened. Virginia resorts to fawning and talking too much about complete irrelevancies.

Not-in-control/unresponsive. Bryan defends himself

against threats by self-protection, struggling to keep the waters calm and smooth and avoiding disruption to his ordinary daily routine. He accepts new assignments only reluctantly, and he doesn't want a lot of attention from others. Wishing to be left alone to do his job, he sometimes rages silently when anyone tries to drag him into a situation that could possibly deny him his safety. Especially around Kathy, and at times when Allen needs his input or feedback the most, Bryan clams up. His refusal to communicate throws a major obstacle in the way of the group's success.

Not-in-control/responsive. Virginia natters on to a far different sort of beat. Fearful of rejection, she demands constant recognition and acceptance from everyone, Kathy in particular. Social to a fault, she defuses Kathy's outbursts with flattery and acquiescence. This way she shows how much she cares for others and hopes that in return they'll care for her.

Feeling compelled to preserve her friendships at all costs, even if nothing is really threatening them, she carries being a friend, a colleague, a peer to extremes. This behavior is *controlling* by virtue of the near-hysterical energy it generates, but Virginia exercises little personal power to direct the relationship toward constructive business ends. She creates an obstacle through too much communication that's too often irrelevant.

These are three patterns of difficult behavior you'll find anywhere. As frustrating as they are to you, they're easier to handle than the problems ultradifficult people pose for you.

Ultradifficult People

Ultradifficult people carry troublesome behavior to sometimes neurotic extremes. Their behaviors are inappropriate in *any* circumstance. They may seem to fit into the three troublesome patterns, but they're more compulsive, repetitive, and irrational. They disrupt the best-laid plans, and sometimes, there's nothing you personally can do about it.

One pattern undermines morale: chronic depression. Depressives appear tired all the time. They take a bleak or pessimistic outlook on everything in general and spread gloom everywhere for everyone.

Hyper people create a different environment: too much energy. They can't seem to sit still, stop talking, stop doing things, only some of which are productive. They undermine the group by constant activity, frequently irrelevant and unnecessary.

Manic-depressive people combine both behaviors, but in cycles. Their moods swing up and down; in most cases, that's all. In some cases, however, their mood swings are too severe for others to tolerate and require medical attention.

Finally, look out for game playing. Game players attempt to get their way by substituting the game for rational and direct behavior. Originally identified by psychiatrist Eric Berne, games in this sense are usually *consciously selected behaviors* that appear on the surface to be benign, when in fact they're attempts to undermine effective relationships. They're repetitive behaviors that go on at the expense of or to the detriment of others and end in a payoff for the game player. The most frequent games found in the workplace are called "power play," "gotcha," "let's fight," "uproar," "you and him (or her) fight," "why don't you?" and "woe is me."

Frequently, someone like Kathy engages in "power play." To such people, everyone threatens their authority or their status or the payoffs they want for themselves. They try to block everyone else's advancement or due recognition, often taking the credit for what other people do. They advance themselves at the expense of or to the detriment of other people.

In "gotcha," the game player sets you up for making a mistake, or failing to do a job, or missing a deadline, and so forth. Bryan plays it by not giving the group information it needs and then silently laughing at them when they can't get on with their work. The payoff is a sense of personal power, especially useful to a person who doesn't feel powerful.

"Let's fight" players argue all the time. This is one of Kathy's favorite games. Sometimes it's just innocuous, a chance to crow over a vanquished victim. Other times, she plays her game to control the process. The short-term return consists of diverting attention from everything and everyone else and to the game player.

Often "let's fight" becomes a game of "uproar," in which everyone shouts at each other, achieving nothing other than ventilating feelings. Letting out your feelings when you're angry is healthy, but screaming and shouting at one another goes beyond rational confrontation. The one who outshouts or shouts down everyone else wins.

Bryan finds a variation on "let's fight" amusing: "you and him (or her) fight." He sets up situations that provoke Kathy into arguing with Allen. For example, one time, knowing how volatile Kathy is, he *suggested* to her (though he never actually said it) that Allen had approved adding more salt to one of their soybean recipes. "I know it tastes tart, but I thought Allen wanted it that way," is all he said. Off she went to "tell Allen a thing or two." Again, this game provides a sense of power to those who feel powerless.

Kathy tells a lot of people a lot of things. She plays "why don't you?" Thinking that she knows everything about everything, she's quick with advice and recommendations, whether or not they're requested or received well.

If things don't work out the way she said they should, she then plays "gotcha." "Obviously, you didn't do it the way I told you to." Or if you don't do something she suggests, and things don't turn out well, she says, "I told you so."

Either game or both games taken together—"why don't you?" and "gotcha"—feed the player's ego.

Finally, Virginia has a favorite game also: "woe is me." She particularly likes to play it with Kathy because that gives her a chance to let the more powerful woman play "why don't you?" In a strange way, that gives Virginia a feeling of control; she keeps Kathy giving advice that's doomed from the outset. The name "woe is me" pretty well describes the game. Chronic complaining, chronic weeping—and a chronic refusal to do anything about the situations that evoke the complaining and weeping. The object of the game is to get attention, not to solve problems.

No matter how your difficult people act, you can count on one thing. They are trying to meet needs or reach goals of their own, and you can use that to your advantage when trying to get them to change.

Behavior and Needs

There's a definite connection between behavior and needs. By watching how people act, by listening to what they say, you can *frequently* (but not always) judge fairly well what needs they're trying to meet. For example, constantly seeking the limelight suggests a need for attention or recognition. Hiding from the limelight suggests a need for security. And so on. When you have a better understanding of the whys and hows of the behaviors of difficult people, you can deal more effectively with the obstacles they create.

I'm compelled here to issue a word of caution. All comments about human needs are *inferences*—conclusions we draw about people by watching how they act and by listening to what they say. We see someone do something or hear him or her say something, and we conclude that that person is trying to meet a certain need. We speak conclusively only about what we see, hear, touch, feel, and smell—and even then we're describing only our own impressions or interpretations of those sensory data.

By way of summary, I've designed a diagram of the four patterns (see Figure 1). Notice that in-control/responsive and not-in-control/unresponsive are opposites, as are in-control/unresponsive and not-in-control/responsive. The determining factor in the differences in the behaviors comes from one's ability, or lack of it, to take control of one's own life or of the current situation. Responsiveness refers to *how* one takes or doesn't take control, which is expressed as *extremes* of in-control or not-in-control behavior.

If you're thinking of altering your own behavior or of asking someone else to act differently, then compare different types of behavior, starting with the similarities.

Figure 1. Four Patterns of Behavior

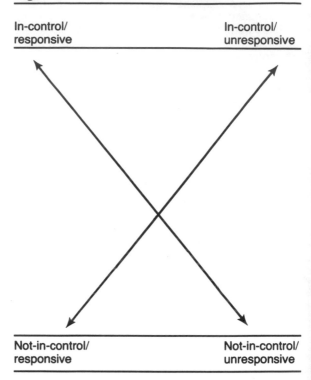

In-control/
responsive

In-control/
unresponsive

Not-in-control/
responsive

Not-in-control/
unresponsive

Do you want to stay in control but become more responsive? That's a matter of adjusting your behavior with relatively little effort. Do you want to get more control—let's say, move from not-in-control/unresponsive? That's a major adjustment.

The diagram is not a change agent but rather an analytic tool for looking objectively at different styles of behavior and their relationships to one another. It also suggests the degree of ease or difficulty you can expect in trying to change your own behavior or asking someone else to change his or hers. In the next chapter, I'll address steps to take to shift your behavior.

Into which patterns does your behavior fall? Take a look at part 2 of the Appendix now, and see for yourself. See whether any of the conflicts with others you experience may originate with something you might be doing or saying. You may be able to correct some of the negativity in your relationships simply by shifting your own gears into proactive behavior.

Difficult People You Know

Now that you've finished reviewing your results, think about the people with whom you experience difficulties. Into which patterns do their behaviors fall? In the sidebar, there's a worksheet with which you can evaluate behaviors, including those you find most objectionable. Use the examples in each box as a model for how to identify the person's behavior style(s).

In the example, Allen's looking at the whole person, not only at the part that drives him crazy, in order to communicate more effectively with her. He lists things Kathy does or says that reflect both forms of in-control behavior, that which is acceptable as well as that which isn't. Hard as it was, he found one thing she does that constitutes not-in-control/responsive behavior, but he could find none in the not-in-control/unresponsive class. His picture of the woman is now both complete and specific.

Develop one chart for each person with whom you're having difficulty. Try to do one on yourself or have a close and candid friend help you. Be specific. *Identify those behaviors you want to see changed.* I seriously doubt you'd get anywhere saying to someone: "I'm not happy with the way you act. Please change."

You should now have a new awareness of your own behavior and that of the people around you. You may create some of the obstacles to good relationships yourself, or a combination of things may produce the problems. Either way, you need tools for changing your own behavior or for dealing with difficult people.

Behavior-Analysis Worksheet

Name: Kathy

In-Control/Responsive	*In-Control/Unresponsive*
Asks for difficult assignments and solves problems. Works without supervision. Organizes work well. Meets deadlines on her work.	Writes demanding memos. Argues in every meeting. Demands the floor first. Gets defensive when we disagree. Calls Virginia a fool. Laughs at Bryan's ideas. Plays power game with me.
Not-in-Control/Responsive	*Not-in-Control/ Unresponsive*
Tells jokes in meetings, usually in bad taste.	

Chapter 3

Changing Your Own Behavior

Changing your own behavior or coping with difficult people takes a great deal of effort and will. Before you begin any program, you need to decide what it's worth to you, the kind of payoff you want to get, and the chances that you'll get it.

A Rational Approach to Change

Labor/management relations experts, consultants on conflict management, and group-dynamics leaders in a variety of fields all use the methods in this book in one form or another. You can call these methods rational because they deal with emotional or irrational issues in a rational way. Still, in an almost ironic sense, their success depends on something relatively irrational: the *willingness* of everyone to give change a chance. That willingness comes when each person sees the benefit to himself or herself of working toward change.

The effort exacts a price, to be sure. You'll probably pay for change with emotional and mental energy— because this book rules out working around people, going over their heads, or manipulating them as actions of choice. Under most conditions, any of those indirect actions signals to other people, including your difficult ones: (1) You can't deal with confrontation, (2) you can't be trusted, (3) you're a game player. Taking indirect action usually invites even more trouble than you had before.

Indirect action produces barriers to improving relations with difficult people unless you use it as—and *only* as—the two-by-four that catches their attention, a *preliminary action* designed to bring recalcitrant people to the discussion table. Then it has some constructive value.

What's It Worth to You?

If you're thinking about changing your own behavior, consider these possible outcomes:

1. No matter what you think about the situation you're creating, you don't want to change your own behavior.
2. You want to change your behavior, but you don't think you can do so in time to make a difference.
3. You want to change your behavior, time's no problem, and you think you know how.
4. You want to change your behavior, time's no problem, and you think this book can help you.

Now consider the possible outcomes with respect to getting someone else to change his or her behavior:

1. The other person will rebuff your initial overtures, and you won't get a chance to do anything.
2. The other person will listen, get angry, and tell you to get lost.
3. The other person will listen politely to your initial overture and then tell you to get lost.
4. The other person will listen and give your plan a try but will then give up prematurely.
5. The other person will listen and give your plan a try, and everything will work out well.

Given all those possibilities, you have to weigh heavily what it's worth to you to try anything at all. Consider this especially if your difficult person is your boss. He or she could just up and fire you. Then it might be the better part of valor either to accept the status quo and suffer, or move to another place in the organization or out of the organization altogether.

How important to you is asking for a change? What's the risk to you? The benefit? Can you continue to live with the situation, if the outcome of direct action could be disastrous for you? Taking *no action* when inaction is your *best* option is a positive step.

Before you run off to make wholesale changes in your own behavior or ask someone else to make that sacrifice, decide whether or not the payoff justifies the effort. What *is* the change worth to you? If it is very important, take all the necessary steps. If it's not important at all, why do anything?

When making a decision, consider the three basic business dimensions that could be affected by the way either you or another person interacts: productivity, interpersonal relations, and stress. How will a change in either your behavior or that of the other person affect those three factors? Will productivity be improved? Will the disruption in interpersonal relations or the stress in the office be eliminated or reduced?

If you're in charge, and the person won't or can't change, what do you do? Fire him or her? But what if his or her productivity is critical to the success of your unit? On the other hand, if he or she doesn't produce well either, what do you stand to lose by firing him or her?

When the need for change puts you on the line, do you care enough about this job to make the effort? How much do you value what you're doing and where you're doing it? If this position means a lot to you, why not make the effort?

The decision comes down to this:

> *Expend the effort to change or to seek a change from the other person when the amount of effort you would expend seems to be directly proportional to the value of the change with regard to productivity, interpersonal relations, and stress in the office.*

Working on You

Making a change in your own behavior requires a greater personal effort than asking someone else to change. And asking someone else to change may require you to straighten up your own act both before and after.

That's what Sara advised Allen. He had withdrawn in the face of Hurricane Kathy. He had retreated to his backup style of not-in-control/unresponsive. Until he works on himself, he can't hope to draw the others into the position of in-control/responsive along with him. He needs to look at why he had retreated—what needs he had been meeting—and then work out ways to move back into control, either by finding other ways to meet those needs or by sacrificing them for his own greater good.

You began your change program when you evaluated your personal behavior style. You saw how you may provoke other people. If ordinarily you're in control and responsive to others, then you probably can cope with the situation fairly handily, with little preparation besides planning your approach to the other person. If you found other tendencies in your main style of behavior, then you have your work cut out for you.

How about one-er behavior—in control and unresponsive to others? Did your decisions in the Appendix exercise fit that style? If they did, then remember that aggressive, unresponsive people don't permit genuine two-way communication. They talk *at* people rather than with them. They don't heed the opinions of others, and they dictate rather than discuss. Begin your effort to change by making a list of things you can do to alter the pattern: Listen attentively, acknowledge people's feelings, give them credit for their ideas, ask them to do things rather than order them about, and so forth.

If you're planning to ask someone else to act differently also, you'd better guard against a tendency toward aggressiveness. Since a favorite game of in-control/unresponsive people is "why don't you?" you may also have to guard against getting into that situation when asking someone to change. The end result could be a game of "uproar."

Instead of telling someone what to do and how to do it, collaborate with him or her on some problem solving. I'll show you how in the next chapter.

What if you found yourself to be unresponsive but

not in control? On the chart of opposites, you saw how long is the road to change between there and in-control/responsive. What you're doing now is a form of withdrawal or retreat from dealing with other people up front. You may even be a bit hostile toward them. Security or safety dominates your actions, and at times you could even engage in a game of "you and him (or her) fight"—or sometimes you feel like instigating it.

Changing your own behavior or asking someone else to change might be pure torture for you right now. Yet you might decide it's worth it for you to change or to take some other action, since you're experiencing some kind of pure torture now anyway. Might as well torture yourself in the name of change. Becoming more responsive to others may be the best next move to make.

Sliding to the left a little could get you moving on track: listening to people with interest and warmth, engaging in real dialogs instead of withdrawing behind folded arms and a glazed look, taking a few social risks (reaching out to others). By becoming more responsive, you may not have to ask anyone else to change. The change in your behavior may get them to act differently toward you, as well. At the same time, from this starting point you can move toward getting control of the world in which you live and work. Just be careful not to move too far to the left and stay not-in-control while becoming too responsive.

Of course, if you're starting from not-in-control/responsive, you realize that you have to be on guard against being too solicitous, too friendly, too ready to agree, too ready to give up your own causes. Move to the right, but just a little. You'll accomplish more by backing off your current tendencies, but you don't want to become altogether unresponsive.

If you think you talk too much about irrelevant things, you'll have to put a lid on it. It'll be hard for you, but if you decided it's worth it, then the payoff will justify the work.

If you intend to ask someone else to change, you could make the whole idea appear trivial by playing down the importance of the issue to you. Taking control means letting your needs and their importance be known. You want people to take you seriously.

Whatever your dominant behavior style, you can change it, if you want to, by rereading the section on in-control/responsive behavior and, as best you can, adopting those proactive moves. Then, combine them with the communication techniques you'll read later on in this book to accomplish the goals you set for yourself.

Working on Other People

Let's eavesdrop on Sara and Allen a moment. Advice well taken has led the team leader to reconsider his lack of assertiveness. Still, he has some reservations about what he now has to do. In their conversation, Sara and Allen pretty well spell out what expectations you should carry with you when you consider asking someone else to change:

Allen: I'm a biochemist, not a psychologist. I can't make over those people.

Sara: I should hope you *can't*. No one can make over another person's basic personality. They can't even do it to themselves, really. Most psychologists admit that, but you can help them work toward changes in the behaviors that are getting in everyone's way.

Allen: I'd be happy to achieve a truce—an accommodation until this project's over.

Sara: That may be all you can hope for. But I think you've made a good start by planning what you have to do about yourself to get their cooperation. By taking an assertive stance, you'll cope better and lead them into new patterns.

Let's dissect Sara's last remark. It contains the three points you need to consider if you plan to become a change agent.

1. *Take an assertive stance.* That means recognize your right to express yourself about a poor or damaged relationship. Simultaneously recognize the other per-

son's right to reject your viewpoint and your plan for change. Be prepared to state your case, but be prepared to negotiate, as well.

Assertive is not aggressive. Most people confuse the two. Aggressive means in-control/unresponsive. Aggressive people don't confront. They attack with name-calling, blame, and demands. In the process, they alienate other people.

Assertive means in-control/responsive. When you confront someone assertively, you claim your rights, but you use warmth as a way to sustain the other person's self-esteem in the process. Remember, no one's "all bad," and if you support the other person's self-worth, he or she will be more likely to work with you.

2. *Cope with the behavior.* That means accept the fact that the person's personality may be set in concrete, but in the name of mutual benefit, he or she may be willing to act differently when around you than when around other people.

Part of helping the other person meet his or her self-esteem needs comes from accepting the other person for what he or she is, valuing the other for those positive characteristics he or she brings to the table. You don't have to like someone in a social sense to work well with him or her. You need only respect him or her as a person or as a professional and get respect in return. Sometimes, once a difficult person experiences respect, he or she looks deeper inside to find ways to become likable, too.

3. *Lead.* In *How to Be a Successful Manager,* another book in this series, I defined leadership in management as

> the ability to mobilize the energies of other people toward the achievement of a goal or an objective that may or may not be in their own best interest.

In this context, I alter the definition in only one small way:

> . . . a goal or an objective that they may not at first perceive *is in their own best interest.*

A small but significant modification.

The first definition implies that managers ideally should try to get people to see that doing a specific job is in their own best interest. If they don't, it doesn't matter as long as the job gets done. The second definition says that you have to emphasize people's best interest because, in this context, you're asking them to make changes in what they do and say. Especially if you're not their manager, unless you can sell them on "what's in it for them," you'll never get people to budge off their standard response: "That's just the way I am. Take it or leave it." An effective leader has to sell the benefits, or the desire to change won't materialize.

That's the irrational part of this rational system. What people see as their own advantage rarely comes from business facts or goals. People work for money not for its own sake but rather in order to satisfy other needs with it—food, clothing, shelter, transportation, and whatever luxuries turn them on. They work for the challenge or for the security or for the social relationships they can get from it. To get someone to expend the maximum amount of effort to do something— especially something as radical as changing his or her behavior—the benefit must fit the person. Only then will the benefit act as a positive reinforcement of the activity or for maintaining the change.

Allen wouldn't enter into a discussion with Kathy saying: "Listen, you're too argumentative. If you'll be less belligerent, we can get more accomplished in our meetings." Kathy would probably answer, "When I'm right, why shouldn't I argue?"

Instead, he might say something to this effect: "Kathy, listen. We all appreciate the technical skill you bring to our meetings, and we want your opinions. However, when you argue with people the way you did with me yesterday, you often cut off different view-points. The others feel put down and don't take all your opinions seriously. Now I know that's not what you want. So I think that we need to talk about how to get other people both to accept your views and to cooperate with you more. How do you feel about talking things over with me?"

It's wordier and takes longer to say, but leaders, whether or not they're officially *managers,* take the time. They plan ways to help difficult people understand that by making an effort, they can achieve their personal goals, too. By watching behavior closely, as I said earlier, you can infer some of the needs that people try to satisfy by acting in the way you find obnoxious or obstructive.

Offering to help the other person satisfy his or her needs, or suggesting ways of getting them met more readily, gives you a trade-off for a change in behavior. "You do this, you'll get that." When the conversation is over, each person feels that the solution to the problem or the plan of action will satisfy his or her needs as best it possibly can.

Allen suggested that by becoming less combative, Kathy would receive the recognition she wants, a genuine leadership position. In return for letting others express themselves without engaging in a fight, she'd have more control rather than less.

What about Bryan? What can Allen say to him? How's this? "You're a darn good chemist, and your suggestion to add more wheat gluten to that mixture paid off. We need to hear more from you, but you seem reluctant to speak up. Then, when you don't say anything, Kathy goads you, and it seems as if you don't know how to deal with that. I'd like you to talk with me about it."

Allen appeals to Bryan's need for being left alone, for protecting his security. Once Bryan agrees to discuss the problem, a plan can be worked out (1) for getting Bryan to become more communicative and show less hostility and (2) for getting Kathy to back off.

And chattering Virginia? Allen tries this: "Ginny, you have something important to contribute to the group. You're the production supervisor, and you know what it takes to get the job done. Sometimes when you're talking, however, it's difficult for me to separate what's important from what's trivial, and we need you as a productive member of the group. I think it's worth discussing. How do you feel about it?"

He appeals to her need for acceptance by the group. However, he focuses on her role in the group as a production supervisor rather than as a friend to everyone, especially to Kathy.

In each case, he supports the team members' self-esteem. He even appeals to their self-image—as valuable, contributing members of the group. Fail to do that, and you lose the ball game before the first pitch. And you can always find something to praise about a person with whom you work. Let's face it. If you can't find some redeeming feature, that person shouldn't be working there.

Sure, it's easy for Allen to pull off these great opening shots. After all, he's the boss. It's easier for him to talk to the people who report to him than to someone to whom he reports. Right? What if your difficult person *is* the boss?

Tough it out, quit, or take a chance on talking with him or her. Those are your options. Going over the boss's head may buy more trouble than it's worth—unless the move's merely a preliminary step. If you decide it's worth it to talk it out, then the approach is the same as that used with anyone else.

What's the benefit to your boss to change? If none exists, which I doubt, accept things as they are or quit. If a benefit does exist, open your discussion with a reference to it. "Mr. Jones, I think you'd like to get more cooperation from me than it may seem I give, and I really do want to be more cooperative. That's why I've asked to see you—to talk about a problem we have between us that I'd like us to solve. How do you feel about talking it over with me?"

You'll sweat, you'll stammer, and you'll flush, but once you get the process started, you'll feel less stress. If it's worth it to you to go for it, try. You have more to lose by letting things go on as they are. The worst Mr. Jones could say in response is: "No, I don't want to talk about it. I just want you to cooperate more."

Now you know there are rational methods for dealing with otherwise emotional or irrational issues. You also know that you have to decide whether the benefit to you is worth the risk from confronting your difficult people. You now know, too, that you may have to work on yourself before you can presume to ask others to change, and you know that if you find the right benefit to fit the person, you stand a chance of enlisting his or her cooperation. What remains is a method for taking advantage of the cooperation you might be able to enlist.

From what you've just read, you can tell that the method of choice for dealing with a difficult person is a direct, well-planned heart-to-heart discussion. How you conduct that meeting spells success or failure.

Chapter 4

Conducting a Heart-to-Heart That Works

A willingness to work on a problem between you and another person requires a voluntary and genuine commitment on both your parts. Solving the problem calls for an investment and involvement from both of you to (1) identify the real problem, (2) resolve any disagreements between you, and (3) design the action plan that can help you both achieve the goals you set. Of course, since we're talking about handling difficult people, you're going to need a couple of sharp tools to get them to conform to the guidelines just enumerated: giving effective feedback and using effective listening skills.

Giving Effective Feedback

Each of the statements I put in Allen's mouth in the previous chapter contains a bit of feedback. Usually expressed as "I-statements," feedback tells other people what you feel when they do or say something that affects you in some way. Naturally, it works the other way around, as well. During a feedback session, or at another agreed-upon time, they give you feedback, too.

Since Kathy presents Allen with his biggest challenge, I'll illustrate the entire feedback process with a dialog between them. This format allows me to insert comments that identify what's going on as it happens.

Behavioral Feedback

You can't get another person to change unless you give him or her feedback that clearly explains what behavior affects you and how. You can't get the change you want unless the feedback also includes what you'd like to see happen.

Feedback statements begin with "I," not "you," and they focus on you, not on the other person. In short, well-formulated feedback statements describe the behavior, explain its effects, and explain your wishes or needs. What makes feedback formulated this way effective is that it expresses how you see things or feel about them without labeling or attacking other people.

Some people find making "I-statements" hard to do. They're more accustomed to saying, "You're too argumentative," than to saying, "I get upset and have trouble taking your opinions seriously when you argue with me almost every time I say something." The first sentence points an accusatory finger at the other person and challenges him or her. The other person will probably argue back with, "I am not!" Let's see how Kathy responds to the second statement:

Allen: I get upset and have trouble taking your opinions seriously when you argue with me almost every time I say something.

Kathy: I want you to take my opinions seriously, and I don't think you do. I guess that's why I argue so much.

The second statement's complexity makes it difficult to respond with "I am not!" It consists of (1) a problem you're having ("taking your opinions seriously"), (2) a reference to the cause of the problem ("when you argue with me"), and (3) a statement of the frequency of the cause ("almost every time I say something"). Kathy's answer gives Allen the perfect opening to say:

Allen: We really want the same thing. What we have to figure out is a better way of getting it than what we've got now.

An effective feedback session follows tested guidelines, a list of which I've included in the accompanying sidebar. Take a look at them before continuing.

- -

Giving Feedback Effectively

1. Give feedback in a climate of trust and caring, and make it constructive, leading to a mutually satisfying goal.
2. Give feedback only if the recipient will accept it.
3. Express feedback in terms of (a) what you perceive, (b) what you feel, and (c) what you need.
4. When restating another person's remarks or instructions, paraphrase rather than repeat them verbatim (parroting), and check for accuracy.
5. When talking about what the other person does, describe behaviors over which he or she has some control rather than personality traits.
6. Focus on directly experienced and relatively recent behavior rather than on inferences or hearsay.
7. Be specific, limit the session to only one issue, and explain how the behavior affects you.
8. Mix negative and positive feedback appropriately to demonstrate that your issue is the only point of the discussion.

9. Allow the recipient the right to choose whether or not to change and what changes should be made; work together.
10. Be prepared to accept feedback as well as give it.

-- -- -- -- -- -- -- -- -- -- -- -- --

If you follow the guidelines, you should get the result you're looking for when handling most of the difficult people with whom you work. Though it's hard to believe at times, they usually care about you and your feelings—mainly, of course, because they need other people to help them meet their own needs. That's why you use some type of benefit statement to enlist their cooperation—the trade-off I discussed earlier.

The Structure of the Meeting

The structure of the meeting is itself an important tool for moving toward a solution to the problem. You have to plan the meeting carefully. Set goals in advance and communicate them to the other person. Set the other person at ease, laying down the ground rules for success. Draw him or her into a constructive discussion in which he or she plays an active role, and get the other person's commitment to work toward solving the problem.

Since *you* want the change, it's your meeting to control. That requires a plan, beginning with the evaluation of the behaviors you want to see changed that you did earlier. For each action you want to change, identify a different kind of outcome. For example, Allen wants Kathy not to argue as much as she does. In its place, he wants to see her engage in problem-solving activities. That's what he wants. How they'll get it is through their meeting, which he hopes to use as a modeling session.

He also recognizes that the sensitive nature of this discussion demands privacy. No group activity, this meeting must be held behind closed doors. It'll take time, so he sets aside several hours and asks Kathy to do the same. This is how he sets up the meeting.

Allen: Kathy, I need your help in dealing with an issue that's very important to me and to the success of our team.

Kathy: Oh? What does it involve?

Allen: The way we go about solving problems and resolving disagreements. I need your input as much as I'd like you to hear some things I have to say. It'll take a few hours, I guess, so I'd like to set up a meeting with you tomorrow from two o'clock to closing. O.K.?

Kathy: Sure. I do have a few opinions on the subject.

Allen had no doubt that Kathy would have a few opinions. First, he told her he needed her help. She can't resist that. Second, he asked for her input. At the same time, he referred to his needs—the importance of improving their problem-solving methods, the success of the group, his need to say something to her, too. The team leader set up in advance a climate for achieving results. He should get them.

That you should get the results you're looking for implies that you should also know what results you want from the session before beginning. A non-goal-directed discussion of sensitive issues can blow up in your face. You might wind up in a fight, the other person could withdraw (physically or emotionally), you could misstate your position—any number of mishaps could occur if you don't set yourself a clearly stated objective and then make that objective clear to the other person.

Allen will restate his goals in the beginning of the meeting to make the objectives clear to Kathy. His objectives are almost his opening remarks, but not quite. He first needs to set her at ease—letting her know that he's not looking for a fight, that he's looking for help in solving a problem that exists between them.

He also lays down the ground rules, getting her commitment to follow them and to work out an equitable solution. Let's see how he does all this:

Allen: Thanks for meeting with me, Kathy. How's your project coming?

Kathy: Pretty well, I guess. I think I've got the consistency of the mix close to where we want it. But what's the meeting about?

Allen: I'll come to the point quickly, but I do want to take a second to say that you're doing a great job on this product. You're progressing faster than you projected. That's good. Kathy, as I said yesterday, this meeting's important to me because our team has trouble solving problems and resolving disagreements. I can't settle this issue without your help and cooperation.

Kathy: I'll do what I can.

Allen: That's good, because one of the issues involves how we relate to each other and how the group relates to you. I'm not assigning blame, and I'm certainly not trying to pick a fight. You need to know, however, that I get upset and have trouble taking your opinions seriously when you argue with me almost every time I say something.

Kathy: [*Visibly shaken and a bit defensive*] I want you to take my opinions seriously, and I don't think you do. I guess that's why I argue so much.

Allen: We really want the same thing. What we have to figure out is a better way of getting it than what we've got now. Kathy, listen. We all appreciate the technical skill you bring to our meetings, and we want your opinions. However, when you argue with people the way you did with me yesterday, you often cut off different viewpoints. The others feel put down and don't take all your opinions seriously. Now I know that's not what you want. So I think that we need to talk about how to get other people both to accept your views and to cooperate with you more. How do you feel about talking things over with me?

Kathy: [*Still shaken*] I don't imagine I have any choice.

Allen: In fact, you do, but I'm hoping you want to try to get this situation under control, too. I can't believe that you enjoy the tension that exists between us and within the group. It certainly doesn't give you the influence you should have.

Kathy: [*Taking a deep breath and facing the situation*] I shouldn't argue with you about this, too. If I do, it would only prove you right, wouldn't it?

Allen: It's not a question of right or wrong, Kathy. It's a matter of what we can do to get our acts together. If you're agreeable to it, I'd like to hear what you think the problem is, then I'll tell you what I think; and where we disagree, I'd like us to resolve the issue and set up a plan to make things work better in the future. In fact, I'd like to use this structure for any disagreement we have. O.K.?

Kathy: [*Heartened*] Sounds good. Let's give it a shot.

Allen's using a method that works well in a variety of settings and situations. It's a four-step process: gatekeeping, exchanging viewpoints, resolving disagreements, and achieving closure over an action plan. The preceding dialog illustrated the *gatekeeping* step. Allen and Kathy are now ready to exchange viewpoints.

Notice that even though Allen is the one who had the complaint, the boss asked for *Kathy's opinions first.* By doing that, he finds out what she thinks about the situation. You read in the first dialog passage that Kathy thinks Allen doesn't take her opinions seriously and that that's why she argues. Allen needs to know more about her opinions or feelings in order to deal with them. Unless he knows all he can find out about her perceptions and feelings, they could come back to haunt him before the meeting ends.

It's hard to ask for the other person's opinions when

you're upset with him or her. It involves several different skills, and once you make the request, you have to
sit there and take it all in. You get behavioral feedback
from the other person that you may or may not want to
hear. You're at risk. You reduce some of that risk by
listening actively—asking questions for clarification,
probing for more information, and giving informational
feedback. Most people find the whole process very
threatening.

However, getting the other person's opinion actually
reduces the threat. A difficult person like Kathy is
bound to argue with your opinion if she hears it first.
One like Bryan will retreat. A Virginia will attempt to
placate you and make up for whatever it is you say
she's doing—whether or not you're actually correct in
your assessment of the situation.

By getting the other person's views first, you set up a
number of favorable, nonthreatening conditions:

1. A lower level of antagonism than you might otherwise have created by giving your feedback first.
2. An opportunity for the other person to ventilate
   existing feelings.
3. An opening for the not-in-control/unresponsive
   types, such as Bryan.
4. A chance to talk—but with direction—for the not-
   in-control/responsive types, such as Virginia.
5. A chance to bring important issues, about which
   you may be in the dark, out into the open.

Just as you put your agenda on the table during the
gatekeeping phase, getting the other person's views
first gives him or her the opportunity to do the same.

Listening to Feedback

1. Give your full attention; clear your mind as well as
   your desk and hands.
2. Have an open mind; be prepared to hear things
   you may not like or want to hear, but that could be
   valuable to you.

3. Ask questions for clarification.
4. Acknowledge that you understand both what the person is saying and what he or she feels.
5. Don't respond to or comment on the other person's point of view unless he or she asks you to; make no excuses for yourself or for what the other person says you did or said; don't be defensive.
6. You don't have to do anything about the situation unless you think a change would be mutually beneficial.
7. If you decide that a change in behavior is in order, work out a mutually beneficial plan of action.

Listening to feedback works better if you follow the rules I've included in another sidebar. When you've read these guidelines, I'll take you into another part of the discussion between Allen and Kathy to show you some of the listening tools Allen uses.

Notice that the really important part of receiving feedback is your willingness to *listen*. Not to defend yourself. Not to give reasons. Not to retort. The best way to listen is to attend to everything the other person is saying and actively participate in the conversation, focusing on his or her issues rather than on yours.

Listening Actively

Most people don't listen very much to what other people say, not because they don't want to but because they don't know how. When they do listen attentively, it's usually also passively, and they let many misunderstandings leave the room with them. Through the proper use of questions, informational feedback, comments, and pauses, active listening involves you in the other person's conversation while enhancing what he or she has to say.

Questions for getting information or for clarification take two forms—*open-ended* and *closed-ended*. Open-ended questions can't be answered by a simple yes or no. They begin with *what, why, who, when, where,* and *how*—the questions good journalists ask. When you want to know what a person's thinking or feeling, when you want all the information you can get, you use open-ended questions. Since these questions encourage people to talk and to speak freely, they work well in drawing out a not-in-control/unresponsive person.

When you want to confirm an idea, verify a fact, or end a part of the conversation, you use closed-ended questions. These questions can be answered by a simple yes or no. They begin with words such as *will you, can you, did you, is it,* and *are they.* Since questioning this way discourages people from talking, it works well to keep a not-in-control/responsive person focused and relevant.

Avoid leading questions like the plague. A leading question consists of phrasing a closed-ended question by filling in the answer you want to hear. The other person would feel stupid or silly if he or she didn't agree with you. For example, Allen could have said, "You want people to accept your opinions, don't you?" Thank goodness, he didn't say that. Kathy might have exploded at him.

Not only questions keep people talking; other devices can do the same thing. A simple nod of the head or a brief "Yes, I see" (*gatekeepers* that encourage the other person to continue) show that you understand. *Open-ended comments*—"Tell me more about why you think I don't take your opinions seriously"—get people to open up without feeling you're putting them through the third degree. *Closed-ended comments,* on the other hand, help confirm or verify information—"Then you're talking about my remark yesterday."

Putting the other person's ideas into your own words and checking to see whether you stated his or her case properly (giving *informational feedback* by paraphrasing) does a much better job of confirming your interpretation of what the other person is saying than does a closed-ended comment. Informational feedback takes several forms.

First, you can tell the other person what you think

you heard him or her say—"If I understand you, you think I don't take your opinions seriously." Second, you can also tell the other person what emotions or feelings you're picking up from him or her *(mirroring)*—"I can see that what I said has shaken you up a bit." Or third, you can stop the flow of the conversation in order to check out what's happening (a *process check*)—"I feel as if you and I aren't talking about the same things. I'd like us to review where we are to make sure we're on the same wavelength."

The last listening tool, but probably the most important one of all, is the proper use of *pregnant silence,* which makes the whole process work. Deliberately creating dead air (as opposed to being at a loss for words) lets the other person know that you want him or her to speak, that you want to hear what he or she has to say. It works wonders when talking with a Bryan, though the long silences put your patience to a real test. On the other hand, you want to keep pregnant silences to a minimum when talking with a Virginia or a Kathy. They'll take advantage of them to work their will contrary to your goal.

These listening tools work because they force you to give your full attention. They set you up in the other person's mind as an empathetic person with a concern for and interest in him or her. Listening this way reinforces the other person's self-esteem and helps raise that person's receptivity to your views and to working with you to solve the problem.

By the way, if you're attempting to change your own behavior from unresponsive to responsive, developing your active-listening skills will produce a dramatic effect on you and on other people. The follow-up to the listening phase of exchanging ideas, however, can destroy everything you have produced thus far unless you handle it carefully.

I'll take you through the next phase after I've illustrated the first one through another portion of the dialog between Allen and Kathy. As you read along, notice my notations in brackets. They point out how the two of them follow the guidelines and use the communication devices I just covered.

Allen: I'd like to hear more about what makes you think I don't take your opinions seriously. *[Open-ended comment]*

Kathy: You side with Bryan all the time.

Allen: *All* the time? *[Closed-ended question]*

Kathy: Well, often.

Allen: Then you think that I take Bryan more seriously than I do you. *[Informational feedback]*

Kathy: That's right.

Allen: When and how did I give you that impression? *[Open-ended question]*

Kathy: When you accepted his suggestion to increase the level of wheat gluten, for one.

Allen: And others? *[Open-ended question]*

Kathy: Well, uh, there have been other times, too. I just can't remember them all. It's not my style to hang on to bruised feelings.

Allen: So, if I've got this right, you're angry because I accepted Bryan's suggestion to increase the wheat gluten when you disagreed with him. *[Mirroring]* Is that right? *[Closed-ended question]*

Kathy: That's right.

Allen: What else do you want to say about that? *[Open-ended question]*

Kathy: That's it, I guess.

Allen: And you think that my siding with Bryan that time is the reason why you argue with me a lot. *[Informational feedback]*

Kathy: *[She doesn't answer right away, and Allen waits without saying anything; he permits the pregnant silence to encourage the other person to answer, which she finally does.]* Maybe it isn't the only reason. *[More silence]* I . . . uh, I sometimes feel I have to prove myself to get anywhere in this company. If I don't do more and have more successes than Bryan, he'll get promoted before me just because he's a man.

Allen: Go on. *[Open-ended comment]*

Kathy: You know as well as I do there are no women in upper management here.

Allen: You see none up there. [*Closed-ended comment*]

Kathy: Well, no. Do you?

Allen: Sara's a senior manager. In distribution, Alice Blaine's an AVP. But let's save my perceptions for when you're through. I don't want to cut you off in any way.

Kathy: They're exceptions.

Allen: Then, if I understand you, you think you can get ahead in the company by arguing with me, Bryan, and Virginia. [*Informational feedback*]

Kathy: As long as I prove myself right.

Allen: Have you done that? [*Closed-ended question*]

Kathy: Not in every case. [*Pregnant silence*] Especially not in the case of the wheat gluten. [*Pregnant silence*] And not when I thought you wanted the extra salt in the mixture. [*Pregnant silence*] And not when I called Virginia a fool for thinking we should boil the soya beans longer. [*Pregnant silence*] I guess I've been wrong a lot lately.

Allen: What more do you want to add to what you've said? [*Open-ended question*]

Kathy: I think I've said too much already.

Allen: Then you're finished? [*Closed-ended question*]

Kathy: Yep.

That completes phase one of exchanging viewpoints. Allen listened attentively, nonjudgmentally, nondefensively, with empathy—letting Kathy draw her own conclusions about what she had been doing. He never challenged her, though he probed to clarify things she said, even when she made the comment about there being no women in executive management. Until she asked him, he made no rejoinder, and after he answered her question—very briefly—he turned the conversation back to her issues. Now it's Allen's turn, but first he needs to find out whether Kathy is ready to hear his viewpoint.

Allen: Just to make sure we're talking about the same things, I'd like to review what you've said. [*Process check*] You think I take sides with Bryan against you and that the company doesn't promote women into upper management. Those are the reasons you give for arguing with me almost every time I say something. [*Informational feedback*] The way you see things makes you angry also. [*Mirroring*] Is that a fair summary of what you've said? [*Closed-ended question*]

Kathy: Yes, I suppose so.

Allen: Is there something you want to add or correct? [*Closed-ended question*]

Kathy: No. You really do understand what I'm trying to say.

Allen: How do you feel about hearing my viewpoint?

Kathy: [*After a pregnant silence*] To tell you the truth, I didn't think at first I'd want to, but you've been fair and heard me out. I suppose I'd appear unreasonable if I didn't. So go ahead. I'm listening.

Allen summarized her position, making it clear to her that he was listening and that he did at least try to understand her point of view. That opened the door to asking for a chance to speak without jamming it down Kathy's throat. You probably also saw my point about the structure itself helping to solve the problem. Because Allen listened to Kathy first, she was ready to listen to him.

Phase two's success depends on brevity and clarity—on giving effective feedback. Allen points out where he agrees with Kathy. Then he focuses on his feelings and needs, while recognizing Kathy's.

Allen: I agree that I sided with Bryan on the wheat gluten thing. I also agree that Sara and Alice represent only a minority of women in the company. Still, I sided with Bryan only one time, and I have no control over who gets promoted into upper management. So I disagree that either situation gives you sufficient reason to argue with me the way you do. I become quite upset because the arguments disrupt our meetings and interfere with our ability to do any genuine problem solving. We need to get those products to market on time, and we won't be able to do that unless we settle down in our meetings. How do you feel about what I've just said?

That's it. Succinct and to the point. That's really all you have to say. Further exploration of your ideas takes place after the other person answers in phase three: resolving disagreements.

During this phase, you get the other person's opinions or feelings about your viewpoint. You let the other ventilate whatever feelings have been aroused, and you get him or her to help you close a very important gap—the gap between what the other does to meet his or her needs and what you have to have to meet yours. Remember that this gap is critical in understanding what makes a person difficult for you.

Deal with the disagreements by letting the other person respond to them first. Let the other resolve those he or she can before you do any coaching. Then each of you can offer resolutions to disagreements that still remain. Or let them stand if they seem irresolvable—as long as they won't interfere with progress toward a solution to your problem. Notice also that when you're trying to resolve disagreements, you may have to repeat the exchanging of ideas of phase two. You'll see where Allen and Kathy do that in the middle of the dialog.

Kathy: O.K., so I'm wrong about you siding with Bryan all the time, but having just two women in higher levels of management doesn't make for fair policies.

Allen: You're pretty ticked off about the company's promotion policies. [*Mirroring*]

Kathy: You can bet on it. I think it stinks that I have to turn into Wonder Woman just to get ahead

41

	around here. No one expects Bryan to work more than anyone else or harder than anyone else just to get a promotion.
Allen:	Then you think I expect you to excel, whereas I expect Bryan just to be average. [*Informational feedback*]
Kathy:	You've got it, Buster.
Allen:	I see you're still pretty steamed up over this. [*Mirroring*]
Kathy:	[*After a short but pregnant silence*] Oh, Lord. I'm sorry, Allen. I shouldn't have mouthed off at you like that.
Allen:	I'd be lying if I said I didn't mind it, but I think I understand how you feel. I don't agree with you on your perceptions of company policy or my expectations or your right to argue with me at the drop of a hat. I'd like to tell you how I see it, if you'll give me a chance. [*Open-ended comment*]
Kathy:	Sure. Maybe I need to hear this.
Allen:	Kathy, you're a good chemist. No one questions that. Especially not I. So's Bryan a good chemist. Company policy rewards both professional skill and professional behavior. If you never get promoted, Kathy, it'll be because your behavior lacks professional polish. [*Benefit statement*]
Kathy:	The arguing.
Allen:	Not just arguing. Arguments can contribute to growth when they aren't engaged in for their own sake or for winning at the expense of other people. That's what I'm concerned about. I expect both you and Bryan to excel. I won't recommend anyone for promotion unless they do. If I had to choose between you right now, I'd have to pass on both of you— and for similar reasons. What do you think of what I just said? [*Open-ended question*]
Kathy:	I don't know what you're looking for.
Allen:	How well have I explained my views on policy and expectation? Have I made myself clear?
Kathy:	Sure, you don't think policy discriminates

Allen: against women, and you don't expect more from me than you do from Bryan because you want us both to be the best.

Allen: Then it's O.K. if I go on? [*Closed-ended question*]

Kathy: Sure.

Allen: Even if you're right about policy, why jump on my case? I don't make policy, but I could help alter it if it were off base.

Kathy: [*Interrupting*] Let's hold it right here. You've made your point. I agree with you for the most part, but I'm still somewhat unconvinced about policy. That remains to be seen.

Allen: O.K., then. On what are you saying we agree? [*Open-ended question*]

Kathy: You're really on my side with regard to getting ahead. You're not favoring the man over the woman, and you're not a policymaker. Given all that, I really don't have the right to get after you in our meetings. I guess I owe you—and everyone else—an apology. I'm sorry.

Allen: Apology accepted, though one isn't really necessary. Instead, we need to work out a plan for how to prevent this sort of situation from arising again. Since we have a basis of agreement on which to build, and since we both want the same things, what do you think we should do, Kathy?

Since they have reached this level of consensus, they're ready to move on. And Allen is asking Kathy to lead the way. It'll be her decision, her objectives, her action plan. She'll have a greater commitment to it than if her boss spells it out for her. He may insert a suggestion now and again, especially if she asks for it, but the change in her behavior that he wants won't come about unless she produces the answers herself.

The plan starts with the *objective* of overcoming the conflicts or problems you've experienced. It then outlines the *steps or means* for achieving that objective. It also identifies the *contingencies* that could impede progress and what you might be able to do about them.

It even includes *dates for getting back together* to talk about how your relationship's progressing. A plan such as this has a much greater chance of success than merely leaving things with, "I guess I ought to change, and I'll do what I can."

I won't go into the details of a plan for changing Kathy's behavior from in-control/unresponsive to in-control/responsive. It would look very much like what I said earlier. I'll just show you how, in their final remarks, they *achieve closure:*

Allen: Well, Kathy. How do you feel about what we accomplished here today? [*Open-ended question*]

Kathy: Surprisingly good. I thought I'd be angry, but I appreciate the way you handled this meeting. I still feel pretty good about myself even though I was in the wrong about a few things.

Allen: How do you feel about following these ground rules in our meetings? [*Open-ended question*]

Kathy: No doubt about it. They work. That's why I built taking a course in interpersonal relations into that plan we just designed.

That's it. Handling difficult people requires skills in gatekeeping, in listening, in explaining your views using effective feedback, and in resolving differences in order to design a plan that works for everyone. And don't forget, I said it would work on your boss, too. It all depends on the willingness of each party to work together.

What This Approach Won't Do

No one approach for handling difficult people works in all cases and at all times. This rational system works most of the time, especially with people whose behavior fits into the three troublesome but typical patterns you've seen. Even then, some people refuse to accept responsibility for creating the conflict—either because they just can't see it or because part of the problem is that they are extremely stubborn. You can't turn everyone into a willing partner to create change.

That's particularly true of ultradifficult people. In fact, that kind of behavior may not always be amenable to solution by a discussion such as the one Allen and Kathy held. Make an attempt, but if it fails, take other action. Irrational behavior can be too neurotic for you to cope with.

In this case, going over someone's head is an appropriate *first* step. The person to whom you both report or, if your problem's the boss, the person to whom he or she reports may be able to take steps to get that person to seek professional help. The personnel department of your organization may have access to such outside resources. Check it out, but be pretty sure you're in the right in this situation. The person may just be difficult for you, and that may not be sufficient grounds for anyone else to take action on your behalf.

Be aware also that your attempt to arrive at a solution may make the situation worse. Much depends upon how you handle it, how the other person perceives your attempt, and what the person's status is. Remember, your boss could fire you.

When approaching your boss, test the waters carefully before being too open and candid with him or her. Decide then whether or not it's in your best interest to confront him or her. Be prepared to accept the status quo, as I said earlier, if it's not.

Not only can your boss fire you, if you're the boss and you confront your employee, he or she can fire you by quitting. You may let the employee go, if this individual refuses to change how he or she relates to other people. That's tough to handle if the person is an otherwise good employee (for example, if he or she is extremely productive). In that case, too, you may have to accept the status quo if you can tolerate it.

Just as your employee can take his or her skills elsewhere, a supplier or customer may take its business elsewhere, too. Make your decisions very rigorously.

Conclusion

Analyze, Decide, and Act

The end boils down to this. Most people get along pretty well with one another. Most relationships that don't work well are amenable to resolution. First, identify the problem and who's causing it for whom. Is the other party the difficult person, or are you?

You also have to measure the worth of making an attempt to change either your behavior or the other person's. If it's worth the effort, go for it. If it's not worth the effort, then either resign yourself to the status quo or remove yourself from the situation. (If you're the boss, all you have to do is fire the person for cause.)

If you plan to change your own behavior, keep in mind that the most effective behaviors in interpersonal relations are in-control/responsive. People relate best to those behaviors because they provide leadership while supporting everyone else's sense of worth or self-esteem. Especially in an office setting, that behavior style should be everyone's ultimate goal.

When you decide to try asking another person to change, plan carefully, and use tact. Ask for a well-structured feedback session to work out the problem, and use all your listening and feedback skills. In the end, handling difficult people boils down to resolving the differences between the payoffs both of you want from your relationship.

Appendix

Self-Evaluation

Instructions for Part 1

In this exercise, identify how you might respond to a situation by rating the possible responses to each scenario as to the likelihood that you might respond that way. The higher the rating, the more likely you would do or say what the item describes.

Place your numerical rating in the space provided in front of each response. The ratings should total 8 points. The first scenario serves as a model for how to do this. If no one response describes exactly what you think you would do, rate those that come the closest to it. Be sure not to leave any situation unanswered. And be candid. No one will see this but you.

After you complete part 1 of the exercise, return to the text. Do not read part 2 until the text instructs you to do so because the material there will make very little sense to you at this time.

Exercise

1. You are the manager of a department, and one of your more reliable, productive employees comes in late every morning for a week. You would:

     _3_   a. Cover for him or her in your tardiness reports even before finding out the reason.

     _0_   b. Reprimand him or her in front of everyone in the group as an object lesson.

    _4_   c. Call the employee aside and find out what's been happening, remind him or her of the company policy on tardiness, and work out a solution to the problem.

    _1_   d. Do nothing, hoping that whatever problems he or she has will work themselves out.

2. You're in a meeting with people from a variety of departments working out a set of new procedures for handling customer complaints. Someone proposes an idea that you think is utterly silly, but no one else says anything against it. You would:

    ____   a. Make a joke about it but go along with the group.

    ____   b. Tell the person and the group how silly you think the idea is and offer a counterproposal.

    ____   c. Raise questions about the idea and stimulate a discussion that could resolve the problems you see inherent in the idea.

    ____   d. Say nothing at all, hoping the idea falls apart.

3. When you attend a meeting in which everyone seems very serious and intent on what's happening, you would:

    ____   a. Try to liven things up by telling a few funny stories or making small talk.

    ____   b. Try to push everyone to finish up the meeting as fast as possible.

    ____   c. Participate with the level of seriousness and intensity appropriate to the situation.

    ____   d. Back out of the group as gracefully as possible.

4. You're in a department meeting, and someone failed to provide some available and important information the group needs for solving a problem. Its absence has created tension in the group. You were not responsible for gathering that information. You would:

___ a. Try to relieve the tension by making light of the situation, telling everyone how you've seen this sort of thing happen before and that it works out in the end.

___ b. Demand to know who failed to get that information and make an issue of its being missing, pointing out that the group's effort is stymied by that person's failure.

___ c. Acknowledge the importance of the information and volunteer to get it quickly—immediately, if possible.

___ d. Do nothing, but get some quiet satisfaction from everyone else's discomfort.

5. When you come into the office in the morning, you like a fresh cup of coffee. Frequently, though you're on time to work, other people get there before you and empty the pot before you can get to it. They don't always make another pot, and you have to make the coffee before you can have a cup. You would:

___ a. Make jokes about it to everyone but continue to make the coffee without any serious discussion.

___ b. Try to find out who's taking the last cup without making another pot and have it out with him or her right there and then.

___ c. Discuss the situation with the other coffee drinkers in the office and see if you can't come up with a plan for solving the problem.

___ d. Get to work as early as possible, say nothing to the other coffee drinkers, but silently seethe at them.

6. Your boss is making you the butt of a joke in front of the rest of the department because you made several serious errors the day before. You're very embarrassed and uncomfortable. You would:

___ a. Join in the joke making and laugh along with everyone else.

      b. Get very angry and tell him or her to stop immediately or you'll walk out.

      c. Acknowledge your errors, and when the meeting is over, ask your boss for a private meeting to discuss your feelings.

      d. Do nothing and silently wish your boss the worst possible day.

7. You've had some personal problems at home, and you're not feeling up to par. Several other people have had to take over a share of your responsibilities to get the work done on time. This has been going on now for the better part of a month. They come to you to inquire as to what's happening. You would:

      a. Apologize, making light of the situation, and promise to do more of your share.

      b. Tell them to leave you alone, to mind their own business; you'll work out your problems soon and get back on track.

      c. Level with them about your problems at home and ask them for their patience and advice on how to get back on track at work.

      d. Say something to the effect that you have trouble at home and that you'll work things out without their help.

8. You have a co-worker who can't seem to get along with the boss. He or she spends a lot of time complaining and whining about the problem. You would:

      a. Try to cheer the co-worker up, taking the other person to lunch once in a while, doing some of his or her work, and so on.

      b. Give him or her advice on how to handle the boss.

      c. Listen to the problems and help the other person think them through until he or she comes up with ideas for correcting the situation.

     ____ d. Ignore the other person.

9. Your boss just hired a younger person than you, one who shows considerable promise for leadership as well as skill in doing the work. There's a good chance that the boss is grooming this person to take over the department soon. You would:

     ____ a. Get as close to the person as possible, making yourself his or her friend.

     ____ b. Do what you could to slow down this person's progress.

     ____ c. Find out what it takes to get a promotion and work toward it or toward another higher position in the organization.

     ____ d. Resent the boss's doing this to you and consider finding another job.

10. You have a chance for a very large bonus if you can exceed your goals by the highest percentage in the group. Only one other person is close to beating you. On the last day of the contest, that person calls in sick; however, something that your competitor started a week earlier pans out during his or her absence. It puts the other person over the top. Only you know about it. You would:

     ____ a. Get all excited about it and call the person as well as the boss, hoping that they would recognize you for your honesty.

     ____ b. Protest to the boss that it shouldn't count because the other person wasn't there.

     ____ c. File the information with the boss and congratulate your co-worker.

     ____ d. Hide the information until the contest is over.

11. Your boss has asked you to develop a new reporting system. It's quite complicated and takes a great deal of attention to detail and skill. You finish the job ahead of schedule, it's adopted throughout the company, and you're rewarded. You would:

     ____ a. Make light of your accomplishment.

　　　　　　 b. Tell everyone how hard the job was and
　　　　　　　　 that you deserve more recognition than
　　　　　　　　 you're getting.
　　　　　　 c. Feel pleased with yourself and accept
　　　　　　　　 whatever recognition you receive.
　　　　　　 d. Quietly keep to yourself and avoid a lot
　　　　　　　　 of attention.

Instructions for Part 2

You should be on page 15 of the text before you
complete this part of the self-evaluation.

Total all the ratings you have for each item a–d. That
is, total the a's together, the b's, and so forth. Each
represents a different behavior pattern:

a = not-in-control/responsive
b = in-control/unresponsive
c = in-control/responsive
d = not-in-control/unresponsive

When you total them, divide each total by 10. For
example, if you score a total of 6 points for a, the
average is .6. If you score a total of 60 points for c, the
average is 6. And so forth.

Interpretation

Keeping in mind that the instrument has not been
scientifically validated, it suggests that the item for
which you have the highest average score represents
your dominant behavior style. Your backup style is the
one for which you have the second highest score.
Roughly the same average score for more than one
pattern suggests that you tend to split your responses
fairly evenly between them, depending on the situation.

As you've seen from the text, the higher your score
for item c, the more likely you are to get control over
the world in which you work. You probably experience
very little difficulty with the people around you.

Higher scores in any of the other three categories could mean that you may be producing some of the difficulties you're experiencing. Now that you know that, you may want to alter some of your behavior before asking anyone else to change his or hers.

INDEX

ABOUT THE AUTHOR

Donald H. Weiss, Ph.D., of Millers' Mutual Insurance in Alton, Illinois, has been engaged in education and training for over 26 years and has written numerous articles, books, audio cassette/workbook programs, and video training films on effective sales and supervisory or management skills. He speaks regularly on stress management and other personal development subjects, and has produced a variety of related printed or recorded materials.

During his career, Dr. Weiss has been the Manager of Special Projects for a training and development firm, the Manager of Management Training for an insurance company, the Director of Training for an employment agency group, a training consultant, and a writer-producer-director of video training tapes. He also has taught at several universities and colleges in Texas, including the University of Texas at Arlington and Texas Christian University, in Fort Worth.

Currently, Dr. Weiss is Corporate Training Director for Millers' Mutual Insurance.